getting
a better job

JOHN COURTIS

John Courtis, FCA, MIPD, is well qualified to offer advice on getting a better job. He has been in the recruitment business since 1967, as a director of Reed Executive Ltd and, for over two decades, Courtis and Partners, which he founded to provide the full range of resourcing options, including advertising, search and networking. He is currently on the executive committee of the Federation of Recruitment and Employment Services (FRES) and of the Association of Search and Selection Consultants. He is a past chairman of both the Recruitment Society and FRES. In his spare time he writes, with over a million words in print so far, including more than a dozen management books.

Management Shapers is a comprehensive series covering all the crucial management skill areas. Each book includes the key issues, helpful starting points and practical advice in a concise and lively style. Together, they form an accessible library reflecting current best practice – ideal for study or quick reference.

The Institute of Personnel and Development is the leading publisher of books and reports for personnel and training professionals, students, and all those concerned with the effective management and development of people at work. For full details of all our titles please contact the Publishing Department:

tel. 020-8263 3387
fax 020-8263 3850
e-mail publish@ipd.co.uk

The catalogue of all IPD titles can be viewed on the IPD website:
www.ipd.co.uk

getting
a **better** job

JOHN COURTIS

INSTITUTE OF PERSONNEL AND DEVELOPMENT

Some of the material in this publication originally appeared in *Getting a Better Job* by the same author, published by the Institute of Personnel Management 1993.

This version first published 1999.

Design by Curve
Typesetting by Paperweight
Printed in Great Britain by
The Guernsey Press, Channel Islands

British Library Cataloguing in Publication Data
A catalogue record for this book is available from the
British Library

ISBN
0-85292-806-8

The views expressed in this book are the author's own and may not necessarily reflect those of the IPD.

**INSTITUTE OF PERSONNEL
AND DEVELOPMENT**

IPD House, Camp Road, London SW19 4UX
Tel.: 020-8971 9000 Fax: 020-8263 3333
Registered office as above. Registered Charity No. 1038333.
A company limited by guarantee. Registered in England No. 2931892.

contents

acknowledgements

First I would like to thank my wife, Dorothy Courtis, MA, MBA, who has been a professional journalist, editor, publisher and writer, in roughly that sequence. She is now also a head-hunter and my partner in Courtis and Partners, so she knows what we are writing about too. Her degree in sociology also helps.

Second I would like to thank Anne Cordwent and her colleagues at the IPD, who have been more than encouraging supporters during this book's gestation period.

Other titles in the series:

introduction

Nearly everyone has to look for a job at least once in their lives. The exceptions – the Dalai Lama, the Queen etc – are in the fortunate position where the job comes to them. The rest of us have either to find a job or to create a job for ourselves.

Whereas once upon a time (and it does seem like fairytale land to those of us over a certain age) people found a job and held it until they retired, most people nowadays have to look for a job several times in their working lives.

This means that if you are reading this book because you are looking for a job, you are doing something almost everybody else has done, is currently doing, or will be doing in the future. The good news is that you are not alone. The bad news is also that you are not alone. There are a lot of people out there, all trying to do what you're trying to do.

What you need is an edge. What you don't need is taking your chances against all the others on a level playing-field. This book is dedicated to avoiding that level playing-field and giving you the attitudes, tools, techniques and understanding to gain an advantage over most of the other players.

This holds true whatever the situation you are currently in. From this position you can tackle the problem of moving from no job to a good one, from a good job to a better one in your current organisation, or from a good one to an even better job in a better organisation.

Getting the leverage to outperform others in the competition for a new job is all about gently making people with the jobs you want fully aware of your strengths. After all, if you don't do it, who will?

There are people who can help you. There are also some who cannot – and some who don't want to. It's important to sort out early on the allies from the people who are a waste of your time. Then you can focus your energies on the task in hand.

That focus, reflected in the plan of this book, is on getting job offers. The good news is that at each stage you have the opportunity to do something that can enhance your position against the competition. Being just 10 per cent better at each stage more than doubles your chances. And some of the improvements recommended in this book won't just make you 10 per cent better: they may transform the results of your application from negative to positive!

Your game plan

To get started, you need to draw up a game plan and stick to it. Use the following steps:

1 Marshal your forces – get the right people on your side to help you with your campaign.

2 Do your homework: research where the jobs are that will be right for you. Find the relevant newspapers and advertisements, and target employers.

3 Produce a good CV, tailored to each specific job opportunity.

4 Write a persuasive and convincing covering letter.

5 Follow up: chase delicately if they don't reply. Obey their further instructions if they do. Confirm interview arrangements crisply and professionally.

6 Make a good impression both before and at the interview. Research the organisation properly beforehand. Then gather the information you want from the meeting and communicate the message you have planned.

7 After the interview, consolidate the good impression you have left and confirm your interest.

8 When they offer, negotiate effectively and warmly. It's your last chance to do this.

9 If they reject you, invite them to keep you in mind for something else.

10 Keep improving your job-search skills until the right offer is made.

1 the people who can help

The people you meet during your job-hunt all have their own agendas and specific commercial interests. It is vital that you understand them so that you are able to use them to your advantage and not alienate them. They can be divided into three categories:

- the professionals
- your own network
- the unprofessionals.

This chapter will deal with the first two groups and provide warning pointers about the third so that you can avoid them wherever possible.

The professionals

It is important to know the difference between the various types of professional firm who purport to help the job-seeker. Terminology varies but includes:

- outplacement consultants
- career (or career-management) consultants/counsellors

- ▲ recruitment consultants
- ◒ selection consultants
- ◓ search consultants (or head-hunters)
- ◉ specialist registers
- ▣ employment agencies.

Outplacement/career consultants

The first two on the list are paid by the individual who is looking for a job (or career change) or by that individual's current/past employer who is returning him or her to the job market. The extent to which these consultants 'place' people varies according to their (declared) objectives and their (undeclared) levels of competence and tenacity.

If you are starting the job-hunt as a result of unemployment, it is almost inevitable that someone will mention outplacement services. Whether you are paying for yourself or your erstwhile employer is footing the bill, you (or the personnel professional involved) should go comparison-shopping first and play hard to get.

This has two advantages. First, it justifies doing the rounds and gathering information without being expected to make an instant decision to buy. Second, the firms you visit will try harder and you, in the course of being sold to, will learn much more about the shades of grey among the various services on offer.

These can range from a slim (even postal) package including tactical advice, help with the CV and some research facilities, through a heavier service with a variety of tests ranging from skill-based or aptitude tests to full psychometric profiling and psychological counselling, secretarial services and practice interviews, to the ultimate all-found exercise in which they write your letters for you, collate advertised vacancies and generally mollycoddle you so much it could sap your initiative. Although help with letters and CVs can be useful, beware the slick, stylised versions that are so instantly recognised – and detested – by employers and others in the recruitment sector.

Research generally suggests that most people get their next job at a senior level not through replying to advertisements or approaching employment agencies and consultants but through careful and appropriate cultivation of their own networks, thereby achieving direct contact with the future employer. Yet the enquirer will often find that one of the major services offered by outplacement or career consultants is the machinery to approach every possible recruitment consultancy or reply to every possible advertisement. In the light of the research, this may not be the best use of your time.

Here are some other things to check out:

● What services are on offer? How do they differ from their competitors'?

■ What results do they claim – both overall and for your type of situation? Look at percentage success, duration of process, salary level achieved (past compared to new, up, down, sideways).

▲ Does the employer-client get progress reports?

● What sort of quality audit/assurance/control is used?

● What is their consultants' training programme? Can you see the training manual?

● Will you get consultants, part-time associates, or franchise associates? Have these people had real experience as employers?

■ How many chartered psychologists are on the team? Are they using trained test administrators and assessors?

▲ Do they follow the relevant Institute of Personnel and Development (IPD) code of practice? Can they even find a copy?

● Will their mixture of one-to-one and group work suit your needs?

The established players are generally well known to practised personnel professionals. Don't assume that the most visible are necessarily the best. It may be that those who advertise least have least need to advertise, most of their work coming through recommendation.

Recruitment/selection/search consultants

Recruitment consultants, selection consultants and search consultants (or head-hunters) exist purely and simply to fill jobs for employers. They do not exist to find jobs for people and most will utter shrill cries of alarm (or worse) if you do not understand this. These consultants have for several decades operated in a market-place where there are more candidates than jobs, so they have no need to be interested in you unless you happen to be relevant to a current vacancy or fit their mainstream specialisation.

Registers/agencies

Agencies and the various registers generally sell people on a fee basis to employers. In normal market conditions they want you as an item of marketable value, and so will be delighted to meet you if you are a worthwhile candidate.

Good agencies will offer you to a client only where you match a known job or a client's long-term needs. Others, where staff are hard-pushed to meet their quota of interviews, may press-gang you towards any organisation weak enough or desperate enough to see you. Average agencies will try quite hard to discipline employers into providing enough data to ensure a good match but may weaken and arrange marginal meetings rather than disappoint you or the employer. You may have to stand your ground.

First, check out with friends the agencies you are considering in order to find out which treated them well. Then give this select few a good CV (be prepared to tolerate application forms) and tell each agency nicely which jobs you are prepared to consider – and which you aren't. If you are firm but reasonable they should not take offence. If you have the courtesy to respond thoughtfully and give your reasons briefly, you will put yourself in the select minority of their preferred candidates – and, if you have misunderstood, they can convince you.

If they react petulantly or sulk, find another agency. If they are members of FRES (the Federation of Recruitment and Employment Services), this offers some guarantee of good practice, because it means that firms have committed to meeting the Federation's ethical standards. (Approaching FRES direct via their Jobseekers' Helpline – 0800 320 588 – and asking for a list of companies that deal specifically with your target area is also a good idea.)

Carefully applied, these filters should reduce your worthwhile agency and consultancy targets to between one dozen and a few more at most. This brings several bonuses. Your analysis of their advertising, backed by up-to-date input from your colleagues and by information gathered from friendly personnel people, should lead you to those for whom you are likely to be of most interest as a commercial opportunity. This would not have been the case for the many more you will have eliminated.

Second, you have now freed up time to approach real employers rather than irrelevant intermediaries. This is important because:

● employers are the only people who can offer jobs – intermediaries can't

■ the jobs that the intermediaries know about are usually only a small percentage of the total available

▲ volunteers who cost employers nothing to find may appear more attractive than those who carry an extra recruitment fee.

If employers like you, they can create a job for you. Intermediaries cannot – unless, of course, you're prepared to cross the desk and join the recruitment industry!

Your own network

If you are fortunate enough to have been in steady employment for half a dozen years or more, you may feel that your network has withered on the vine through lack of regular nurturing or has become too small to be of much use. Don't despair! Provided you don't ask for a job, most of the people you've ever worked for or with or met professionally may be willing to exercise their minds on your behalf or spare time for discussion if correctly approached. This means asking them questions they can answer and being considerate about their time.

The extent to which you can ask for advice or help depends on three variables:

● the closeness of your existing relationship

■ your contacts' perception of how much they can help (you can influence this with a clear letter)

▲ their time pressures.

Your approach will therefore vary from 'Help! I'm desperate,' (which would be perfectly appropriate for a good friend) to the more formal 'Could you spare me a little time to advise me of anyone you know who might want to use these skills later in the year?' And each contact will be sensitive to crowded diaries.

Do speak or write to people personally. Don't be tempted to let a friend or relative do some of the legwork for you. It's lazy and does not make a good impression.

The unprofessionals

They exist. They will not help you. For fear of libel laws, apart from the above pointers, all we can say is *Caveat emptor* ('Let the buyer beware!').

2 where the jobs are

It is important that you address yourself largely or, with luck and good judgement, exclusively to those people who are able to hire you or help you towards your goal. This may appear obvious, but sometimes it is difficult to sort out the sheep from the goats, especially if there is pressure on you to 'maximise contacts'. That is unlikely to be a good strategy.

Identify the real targets

Don't waste your time and energy on people who cannot help you. You need to sort out who has jobs to offer and who has the right kind of contacts with people who have jobs to offer; in other words, identify the principals and their agents – and ignore the rest.

The difference between agent and principal is often blurred in job advertisements and even, sometimes, when you get further down the line. The person you have written to may turn out to be a lowly employee or may be your future boss, a consultant with little authority or a direct route to the attention of the decision-maker. Always try to find out which, without appearing difficult or nosy. Then you can ensure that your approach is tailored correctly to the individual and neither patronises nor antagonises.

Although it might appear that dealing through an agent ought to be less satisfactory for you, it can have advantages. For example, once you have achieved some degree of rapport with a consultant or other intermediary, you can find out which bits of your track record are likely to be of most interest to the client, and you can discover more about the client. It is in the consultant's interest as well as yours that you be properly briefed, and you should find a reasonable amount of background (if not inside) information forthcoming.

Fine-tune your targets

The better informed you are about your target companies, the better you can demonstrate the match between your track record and their needs. This takes time and spadework, but help is at hand if you know where to look.

There is a wealth of free information available to help you do your research. The Internet gives you access to an enormous database (including lots of job-sites: *Monster Board* is just one – www.monster.co.uk). And if you don't have access to the Net from home, public libraries and Net cafés offer excellent facilities. Not yet Net-friendly? Teenage children (your own or those borrowed from other people) make fine and willing guides!

Paper-based sources also abound. These range from such standard reference books as *Kompass* (ie *UK Kompass Register: The authority on British industry*) to *Extel* cards and annual reports (published by *The Financial Times*). Your local public library or area reference library is likely to have *Kompass*, whereas larger organisations and specialist business libraries will have *Extel* cards. You can get annual reports direct on request from the company secretary (useful, if your enquiry will not produce alarm or gossip). Otherwise, invest a small amount in a company search provided by a specialist company for discreet access to the relevant information. Don't forget trade unions, whose central offices have information sections and will know the company's reputation *vis-à-vis* its workforce.

Your own network (or its spin-off network) may also be able to supply useful background data. Somebody will know a good stockbroker or financial specialist with opinions about a company's financial performance and future stability. Others may know someone who works there, or who is a competitor, supplier or customer. Each contact will know something useful. And if you have a rich relative with a diverse share portfolio, he or she may be able to produce annual reports, circulars from brokers and other interesting snippets.

It can also be helpful to visit the shops or showrooms where your target company sells its products. You'll gather invaluable atmosphere as well as information.

How to spot the warning signs

Everyone makes mistakes. Everyone has stories about the disasters (and the monsters) they discovered after they joined a new company. And so everyone – recruitment consultants, investors, suppliers and real people (ie candidates) – will have a special interest in identifying the bad companies to work for and the companies most likely to go bust.

The dodgy company poses a three-fold threat for the hapless candidate who joins it. First, the candidate will be back on the market like a boomerang; second, the candidate's good reputation may be tarnished by association; third, and worst, his or her judgement in joining such an outfit may be called into question.

Danger signals identified by leading industry specialists include:

- lavish HQ buildings (beware especially those with flagpoles, fountains and statues)

- bullying chief executives (to spot these, read *Private Eye* or watch out for brokers' analysts being fired if they criticise)

- complex group structures, especially offshore

- changes of year-end and company name, and several directors

- companies whose directors have made substantial share sales

- those where you can detect creative accounting from the notes to the annual accounts (see below)

■ those where the financial director is out of date – and the accounting systems too

▲ key directors who wear bow ties, gold medallions, toupées and very dark glasses (unless on medical grounds)

● those where the staff are all under 22 in a business where experience and contacts count

◉ those where the non-executive directors are non-entities (retired or otherwise) or chums of the chairman or chief executive

● those where the chief executive was a salesman or Young Businessman of the Year, or is also chairman.

As light entertainment, you might like to use the list above as a check-list against those companies you know well that have gone down the tubes recently. And then check out any company you are thinking of joining or doing business with and giving credit to.

If you can get hold of a company's annual accounts, try reading them from the back page. This is on the grounds that all time-bombs, such as deferred and contingent liabilities, will be described (albeit euphemistically) in the notes, whereas their full possible impact will not show up in the body of the accounts.

Don't assume that it's merely sour grapes if the competition distrusts the company you're investigating. There may be ethical and practical reasons for their contempt. Most senior businessfolk mistrusted BCCI, Robert Maxwell and Polly Peck years before their respective downfalls. Hearing the worst about a company is always better *before* you join!

3 the good cv

Your CV is a marketing document and you are the product you are marketing. Before you create your CV, therefore, you should be clear about your unique transferable skills and the advantages that exist for a new employer in selecting you over the tens (or hundreds) of other applicants.

It helps to think how *you* would feel about being on the receiving end of a hundred-plus applications – and to remember that yours has got to be better. Put yourself in the top 10 per cent with something crisper and more relevant than the competition. Your aim is to avoid the reams of unconsidered tosh that will blur your special edge and simply replicate the rest of the time-consuming applications the recruiter will receive.

Groundwork

Take a large sheet of paper and list all your functional experience – marketing, sales, financial, people responsibilities, etc – down the left-hand side. Then, along the top, list all the positions you've held. Put the job title, company name and sector. This will produce a two-axis matrix. Then mark on your chart with a cross which piece of functional experience was gained in which job.

The resulting clusters of crosses will show you what your functional strengths are and in which sectors and which types of companies you gained the experience. This is the data that will carry most weight with prospective employers. They will be looking for a match between what you have to offer and what they need. This 'broad-brush fit' is the first hurdle you need to successfully negotiate.

Next, flesh out the functional experiences in each job with lists of the competencies, qualifications and significant results that you achieved. Be specific – and, wherever possible, quantify them.

Check out your results with a friendly colleague or adviser. The things that you see as important may not be so attractive to or may even be negative factors for the average employer. On the other hand, the things you don't consider worth much may be the most valuable and rare. You may even have forgotten something important!

Tailoring the CV

If you are applying for a job that has been advertised or been brought to your attention by a consultant, you will be able to work out from the advertisement or job description which parts of your background are the USPs (unique selling-points) you possess for that position. Try to list the hard facts mentioned regarding the preferred candidate and then cross-check your matrix to match these with where you've been and what you've done.

These are the things that must appear clearly in both your CV and the covering letter you send with it. Everything else on your track record needs to be slotted into the CV in an economical way without undue repetition.

If, however, you are approaching an employer or contact directly, you will need to decide for yourself what your personal USPs are and then focus as described above on those.

This approach is particularly good for the reverse-chronological-order CV – where you put your most recent job first. This enables you to devote quite a lot of space to recent achievements and skip the repetitious bits in your earlier career.

Cutting out unnecessary duplication means you can reinforce the impact of the bits you *want* to emphasise by deliberately having them pop up twice, preferably in different words each time. When you put two mentions in the CV together with a brief reinforcement in the accompanying letter, you have achieved the Sam Goldwyn effect of 'What I say three times is true'!

Possible problem areas

Most employers view anything 'different' in your CV with suspicion. This means that any gaps in your career history – eg on account of full-time education, parenthood, ill health or any other reason – should be approached in a direct and positive manner. There's no need to go into detail. Simply drop it into the chronological sequence of your career steps and state what you were doing during that period. If you were able to accomplish anything that will look good for the job you are seeking, don't forget to mention it!

Despite employers' apparent attitudes, in the world of employment everyone is a minority – in terms of gender, race, colour, creed, ability, age and so on. For the better employers who care about meeting anti-discrimination quotas, belonging to a minority group can in fact be an advantage.

There is no absolute obligation upon you to disclose in your CV a disability, whether you are registered disabled or not. Obviously, you have to answer truthfully if there is a question in an application form. But it is best if you can deal with this directly and briefly in your covering letter. Always accentuate the positive: state clearly how your disability does not affect your work performance, so that the employer can concentrate on your skills and experience.

Ageism is another hurdle you may face – at either end of your career! Again, there is no requirement to disclose your age (unless you are asked specifically), but it is always better to inoculate a potential employer so they are not shocked by your youth or silver locks at interview. If you are on the young side for a job, don't mention your age but instead maximise the experience you have crammed into your life, being very specific about the amount of responsibility you have had (both in terms of budgets and people). If you are on the mature side, focus on the recent years and leave out or truncate the earliest stuff. And, in both cases, check that your personal presentation is appropriate for the age-range of candidates the employer is expecting to see.

Explaining the moves

If you have had a lot of past jobs, and the moves were not always of your choosing, don't list every reason why you left each one. You'll make a better impression with a brief paragraph of explanation which says in effect 'I know the period x to y looks a little fragmented, but most of the moves arose from corporate failure, relocation or mass redundancies.'

Make it very clear whether the several companies you worked for briefly were in fact part of the same group. Omitting this will make you look like a job-hopper. Specifying it shows you to be a trusted and worthwhile employee. This is also shown by identifying promotions (make clear they weren't sideways moves), re-hirings, or where your boss has pulled you through to another company when he or she moved.

Calculated omissions are extremely risky. Whatever you are trying to hide, there is nearly always something worse that recruiters will guess at! And if you've used euphemisms, beware: they feel like lies to the discoverer.

CV basics

Don't waste your money on designer CVs. Recruiters are inured to them and they may be a hindrance rather than a help. In general, they reveal more about the designer than the subject. You're probably much better off doing it yourself.

Comprehension tends to vary inversely with the volume of verbiage, so keep it short – but not too short. The one-page CV is unsatisfactory for everyone bar the absolute beginner with no track record, and will probably force you to cram everything onto the page unattractively, perhaps by using a typeface so small that it's impossible to read.

Most recruiters will read two or more pages if the content is good. The first page has to command enough interest (and show enough relevance) to tempt the reader on to the second page and so on.

Don't have a covering page that says only:

CURRICULUM VITAE

Chris Bloggs

In fact, omit the title page and get straight into the real stuff.

Choose plain white or off-white paper. Anything else risks a negative response. That said, designers and other creatives may be permitted some licence. Actuaries certainly aren't.

INSTITUTE OF PERSONNEL AND DEVELOPMENT

Customer Satisfaction Survey

*We would be grateful if you could spend a few minutes answering these questions and return the postcard to IPD. <u>Please use a black pen to answer.</u> **If you would like to receive a free IPD pen, please include your name and address.***

....

1. Title of book ....

2. Date of purchase: month .... year ....

3. How did you buy this book?
   ☐ Bookshop   ☐ Mail order   ☐ Exhibition

4. If ordered by mail, how long did it take to arrive:
   ☐ 1 week   ☐ 2 weeks   ☐ more than 2 weeks

5. Name of shop .... Town.. Country ....

6. Please grade the following according to their influence on your purchasing decision with 1 as least influential: (please tick)

	1	2	3	4	5
Title					
Publisher					
Author					
Price					
Subject					

7. On a scale of 1 to 5 (with 1 as poor & 5 as excellent) please give your impressions of the book in terms of: (please tick)

	1	2	3	4	5
Cover design					
Page design					
Paper/print quality					
Good value for money					

8. Did you find the book:

   Covers the subject in sufficient depth   ☐ Yes   ☐ No
   Useful for your work   ☐ Yes   ☐ No

9. Are you using this book to help:
   ☐ In your work   ☐ Personal study   ☐ Both   ☐ Other (please state) ....

Please complete if you are using this as part of a course

10. Name of academic institution...

11. Name of course you are following? ....

12. Did you find this book relevant to the syllabus? ☐ Yes ☐ No ☐ Don't know

Thank you!

Publishing Department

Institute of Personnel and Development

IPD House

Camp Road

Wimbledon

London

SW19 4BR

Don't waste your money on binders or folders or anything other than a paperclip or a simple staple. Those expensive covers will simply be removed for ease of reading, scanning and photocopying.

Aim for a clear and simple presentation that reveals you as a competent professional. Beware the lure of computer graphics and fancy typefaces that will make your CV look like a Victorian variety-hall songsheet. Instead use bold, italic or underlining very sparingly. And don't put ANYTHING AT ALL in capitals!

Don't put borders of any kind round anything or use reversed-out type (white letters on a shaded background). In fact, don't use shading – it makes photocopying very difficult.

Keep everything 'ranged left' – ie butted up against the left-hand margin – and leave the text ragged on the right side. Leave enough white space between paragraphs to make reading easy.

Bullet points and lists are a very effective way of presenting information. (They also save the bother of writing real sentences!)

Photographs, rather than helping you, will mainly serve to entertain the postroom staff, who will place bets as to whether you're an axe-murderer. At this stage, it's your track record we're interested in.

Make sure that you've made it easy for the recruiter to contact you: specify gender if your given name could confuse; and state whether you can take calls on your daytime phone number, and whether you have an answer-machine on your home phone.

The power of words

Every word in your CV and covering letter will be looked at carefully by the recruiter. You need therefore to scrutinise every word to ensure that each is doing its job properly. Could it convey a more powerful message? For example:

appointed	*could become*	promoted to *or* selected as
site/unit	*could become*	cost centre *or* profit centre
ran	*could become*	created and developed
supervised	*could become*	trained and motivated
closed the…	*could become*	chose to run down the…

Verbs are essential to impact. Look back through your career and think of things that you usually describe in a mundane way but that were in fact examples of how you:

started	introduced	re-established
initiated	created	generated

| developed | trimmed | organised |
| enhanced | tightened up | restructured |

In other words, things that you changed for the better.

Definite don'ts

All recruiters have their personal list of hates. The wise candidate will avoid the most common:

- omitting something we asked for in the advertisement or subsequently – such as salary, age, qualifications – or something basic that we need to know – education, names of key employers etc

- fudging periods of employment, or giving only partial disclosure of qualifications, education or job responsibilities

- using self-regarding descriptions of your charisma, leadership and communication skills (instead of simply telling us you're good, find factual evidence that says it for you)

- trying to be funny: be wry and philosophical if you must and if it's appropriate, but beware attempts at humour

- using jargon – whether of your own profession or that of your career consultant (or that of the – most probably American – book you've read)

- franking your letters instead of using stamps: rather than demonstrating that your outplacement consultant is being helpful, it might suggest an overly relaxed attitude to your employer's property and get you rejected out of hand

- failing to check the documents you're sending out or to use the word processor spellcheck

- getting the recipient's name, job title, address or post code wrong

- getting the job title you're applying for wrong

- using words that you ought to avoid like the plague:

  - charisma/ charismatic

  - leader (especially of men!) *and* leadership

  - résumé

  - commence (*use* start *or* begin)

  - in terms of *or* with regard to

  - challenge (*especially if that's what you say you're looking for*)

  - peruse *or* perusal

- describing yourself as all the things everyone else is:

  - commercially oriented

  - with strong interpersonal skills

△ a good team-player

○ a good communicator

○ profit-conscious (*or at least* cost-conscious)

○ numerate

☐ computer-literate

▣ adopting negative or self-deprecating language

▲ referring to yourself in the third person 'Chris Bloggs is a charismatic leader…'.

Money matters

Opinions are divided about mentioning last salary or salary expectations when writing on spec. If you are approaching an employer direct, it is optional. However, if you are writing to a consultant or an agency, it is absolutely crucial that you tell them what salary range you are aiming at, so that they can consider you for jobs at the right level. If you don't help them, they can't help you!

4 the persuasive covering letter

Job-hunting changes people. When you are applying for a job, you are an *applicant*. You only become a *candidate* if you have applied for a relevant job well enough to make the list of those under serious consideration. The key, therefore, is to turn yourself from just one more applicant into a good candidate. To do this, you must – at least on paper – appear to be in the top 10 per cent worth attention. 'Appear' is the important word. Until the recruiter meets you, you are only as good as your paperwork. And the first bit of paper they see is your covering letter.

'Ah, yes,' you think. 'I've got one of those.' We know. We've seen it. We hate it. And it does *you* no good. You are going to need a variety of types of letters. It is completely counter-productive to try to make do with one. After all, you will probably be sending letters that relate to three different situations:

1   a response to an advertisement

2   a speculative, cold or tepid approach

3   a request for a steer towards a better target

and to three different types of target:

1   employers

2   intermediaries, such as agencies and consultancies

3   influencers through whom you seek to network.

Each permutation demands different ingredients and nuances. To simply post off your CV is the instant route to the wastebin and a lost opportunity to present yourself to advantage. Worse, it may tarnish any later approach.

Likewise, the neutral covering letter ('Please find enclosed my CV...') is also a waste of time, as is 'I am confident that my experience fully meets your requirements' without in any way showing how. This is marketing! You need to make every document, every word, work for you.

The basics

Please have your letter typed. Only ever send a hand-written letter if you are specifically asked to do so. (This usually means that they are going to use graphologists to examine your handwriting – and you need to ask yourself whether you want to work for a firm that believes in graphology.) Note that writing or typing exclusively in capital letters is not just difficult to read; it also casts doubts on your basic levels of literacy and communication skills.

Use plain white or off-white paper. Eye-catching is out. It doesn't work. It's a nuisance to photocopy, scan or highlight. And it doesn't help your chances if you alienate the recruiter from the start.

Research your recipient's address and the correct spelling of his or her name, title and company. Again, the only exception to this rule is if you are applying to an advertisement that requires you to write to 'The Such-and-Such Manager', quoting Reference XYZ. Deviation from the required formula may mean your reply does not reach the correct person or department, gets lost in the corporate postroom or is not recognised as an application for that specific job.

Most letters are best produced to the following format:

- Give your address – not too short, not too long (ie don't abbreviate it so much that it becomes difficult to find you, but don't pad it for effect, either.)

- Give your full telephone number (state whether there's an answer-machine), e-mail address and fax number.

- Address the recipient as 'Dear Ms/Mr [Surname]' unless you know the person well. 'Dear [First name]' is overfamiliar unless you have already met the recipient and are well-enough acquainted to be on first-name terms.

- Provide a heading, underlined and ranged left (not centred), with the reference number and job title if you're applying for a vacancy; otherwise, try for something relevant which will attract attention and lead the reader into the letter. Bland and meaningless headings destine the letter for the wastebin. Examples of these to avoid are:

○ Ref: General Enquiry

☐ Career Move

△ Management Opportunities.

What to say

Get to the point in the first paragraph. Don't waste the reader's time and patience. This is a marketing document, which means you must attract and hold someone's attention. Help the reader to focus. Tempt him or her to read on.

Say why you are writing. Say who you are and what you have to offer. Specify how your skills and experience match the recipient's needs. Then explain how he or she can reach you (phone numbers, answer-machine, voice-mail) and mention, if necessary, good and bad times to make contact.

Use precise words. Avoid opinions and stick to verifiable, and preferably quantifiable, facts. Specify your achievements rather than just experience. And keep it relevant to the advertisement or the reader's interests. Don't waffle.

Even when you are convinced that your record will be understood as relevant by the meanest intelligence, itemise the points that make you clearly appropriate so that the reader is convinced *before* reading your CV. Bullet points are more powerful than rambling blocks of narrative. They catch the eye and present facts efficiently.

Aim for a clean, neat layout with good margins and spaces between paragraphs. And keep the letter to one page maximum.

Sign the letter legibly and, if there could be any doubt about the gender of your first name, try to find a way to make it clear.

Last but not least, use the spellcheck on your word processor and have someone you can trust check it for grammar, spelling, brevity, imprecise words, lack of facts – and appropriate tone. The writer is notoriously the worst person to check his or her own work.

The two sample letters at the end of this chapter are included to give you guidance and inspiration. Most of this may seem peripheral to your suitability for the job – except that your powers of communication are on display. You will not be surprised to learn that failure on the trivial matters can obscure excellence on the mainstream ones.

If you make it difficult for the reader to get a clear picture of you, you may drop back a place in the queue, or even fall off the end! Proper, brief disclosure of the relevant facts, presented well, is likely to attract attention, interest and respect. Anything else is self-destructive.

Approaching a target company – sample

François Braun
Chief Executive
British Group plc
1097 Edgware Road
London
NW29 5AL

[*Date*]

Dear Mr Braun,

I read with interest in this week's *Financial Times* and other newspapers of your Group's expansion plans, as the areas you are moving into match my experience and background. I wonder whether your human resource planning would include a slot for someone like me?

I'm enclosing a copy of my CV, but the salient points include:

- ten years' experience in planning, development and management in your sector

- the most recent five years were with Bloggs Brothers, where I was responsible for regenerating the product line to produce profit improvements of 28% year on year

- tightened credit control, reducing debtors from 87 days to under 60

- I reduced both direct and indirect costs, which resulted in savings of 9% and 14% respectively in the first year

- I restructured the division and initiated staff training, which reduced turnover from over 50% per annum to under 20%.

I am confident that my business experience, combined with my proven ability to develop and improve profit centres, would ensure that I made a significant contribution to your Group.

I would welcome the opportunity to discuss this further with you. I can be reached during office hours on 0207 017 9999 or at the home number given on my CV where there is an answer-machine. I look forward to hearing from you.

Yours sincerely,

Applying for an advertised position – sample

Ms Michelle Jones
Human Resources Director
British Group plc
1097 Edgware Road
London
NW29 5AL

[*Date*]

Dear Ms Jones,

Ref DT/113: Business Development Director, Europe

I read with interest your advertisement in the *Daily Telegraph* on Thursday 26th June for a Business Development Director, as this is a position for which I feel my background is ideal. To preview the information on my CV, let me summarise my strengths and experience for you:

- ten years' experience in planning, development and management in your sector

- the most recent five years were with Bloggs Brothers, where I was responsible for regenerating the product line to produce profit improvements of 28% year on year and was promoted to Business Development Manager

- fluent French and German, plus up-to-date industry contacts in Europe

- before Bloggs Brothers, I spent four years with britEurop plc, working in all of their 14 offices in Europe.

I am confident that my business experience, combined with my proven ability in business development in the UK and Europe, would ensure that I made a significant contribution to British Group plc. My current basic salary is £60,000 with the usual benefits.

I would welcome the chance to meet you to discuss my suitability for the position in more detail. I can be reached during office hours on 0207 017 9999 (secure voice-mail if I'm not at my desk) or at the home number given on my CV on which there is an answer-machine. I look forward to hearing from you soon.

Yours sincerely,

5 managing impressions

Until you actually get to that first meeting, your paperwork carries the main burden of marketing you. Other very important impressions, however, will be provided by your telephone manner – when they ring you to arrange a meeting, and when you ring back.

But apart from any person-to-person conversations you may have, you should also be prepared for the impact of all those other opportunities that people have of hearing your voice and gaining some impression of what kind of person you are. Voice-mail and answer-machines offer opportunities for PR – or pitfalls!

The power of messages

The messages you leave on other people's voice-mail or answer-machines may be more important than any brief conversations you have had with them. This is because those conversations are unlikely to have been recorded. As a result, any trivial clumsy remark you made may have gone unnoticed or been easily corrected. Recorded messages, however, may be played back by a puzzled or incredulous audience unless they are very clear and easy to understand first time round. Particularly bad or strange messages may be played back several times until deciphered (or for general office entertainment) – with resultant incremental damage to your prospects.

Managing the messages

A useful mnemonic is EBB:FLOW, which stands for:

Engage **B**rain **B**efore **P**honing, **L**istening **O**r **W**riting.

Actually, engaging brain before doing anything is better than trying it on autopilot, but do ensure that the little grey cells are on duty before communicating in any way with a potential employer!

To get the most out of leaving messages, you must plan and script what you are going to say. If you have time, it is worth rehearsing it. Remember, there may be only 20 or 30 seconds before your time runs out, so each word must count.

Choose those words carefully. Don't include anything that could be easily misheard, and be especially careful with telephone numbers. For example, should those Os become zeros?

Don't leave peremptory messages demanding that someone call back. The reason for a script is to enable you to leave a coherent message which will elicit a sensible response without the need for further enquiry and more messages.

The perfect message will include:

- your name and telephone number

- who the message is for

- the context (advertisement reference, recent letter, name of contact)

- the message (query, data requested etc)

- what you would like the recipient to do next, or what you will do

- the time by which you or the recipient can, should or may do it.

Anything less than the above will make you sound like a low-tech peasant who will not be welcome on their shortlist.

Even if you firmly believe that the person you're contacting knows you well enough to fill in any gaps, don't risk it – for these reasons:

- The telephone number they've known for years may not be to hand when your message is relayed.

- You may be one of several people with the same surname who are in contact with them at present.

- They are not psychic about your whereabouts.

You may be able to influence their priorities with an explicit message and a reason: for example, could they phone before tomorrow noon because you're flying out to Boston?

Make replying easy. Tell them you have an answer-machine.

Your answer-machine

If you don't have one, get one. They're cheap and it's important that people be able to contact you. If you live in a communal household, negotiate to hijack the answer-machine for the duration of your job-hunt so that it is *your* voice and message that callers hear. Every little helps.

This leads you to the quality of the outgoing message you leave on your answer-machine or voice-mail. It also needs to be carefully scripted – not just because of the time constraint, but because each time someone calls, it offers an excellent opportunity for you to present yourself as professional, thoughtful, reliable, and somebody worth employing. And if you relax and smile as you read your message, you may even come across as a human being!

Always play your outgoing message back and listen critically to how it sounds. And wherever possible, ring in from somewhere else to check how professional – or annoying – the lead-in music sounds. This is your chance to forestall any negative impressions. Remember, the last contact that the potential employer may have with you before the interview might be that dreadful message you left on the machine for your mates on Saturday night!

6 making the interview work for you

If your track record actually approaches the candidate specification reasonably closely and your CV and covering letter are good enough, there is a very good chance that you will get onto the interview programme. Once you have reached that point, emerging from the ranks of the 100-plus applicants into the 10 per cent (or less) of candidates who are going to be taken seriously, your dependence on your CV and covering letter to present your case diminishes sharply.

The paperwork existed to get you the interview. Nearly all jobs are obtained as a result of an interview, so – no interview, no new job. The interview is your next major hurdle.

The onus is on you to perform successfully. There are two things you can do to improve the odds. The first is to improve your interview preparation. The second, especially if you are afraid your interview technique will let you down, is to focus on companies that do test-based assessment of all candidates at your level. That way your true merits will shine through despite your dislike of interviews.

Interview preparation

Time spent in reconnaissance is seldom wasted and, pre-interview, there's a lot you can do. Read the company's annual report and accounts before the first meeting. Extract three or four important issues and learn them. This is not so that you can show off or drag along to the interview a briefcase full of reports. It is preparation for the moment when they ask you whether you have any questions. You will have had the time, and the information, to enable you to respond intelligently.

Review your CV and think well in advance what you will say if they ask why you left previous companies, what kind of reference your last boss is likely to give you and why you want to move. Devise brief sound-bites to convey any negative information quickly and competently in case you are asked.

Do not demand anything pre-interview – for example, detailed instructions about interview location, written confirmation of time of meeting, policy on expense payments or even a job description. The interviewer should provide most or all of these as a matter of course. If they don't, you can ask politely, but never demand. It helps if you are quietly reliable about everything, such as interview timing and sending things you've been asked for or have promised.

Plan your route to the interview and allow a safety margin so that you can be sure not to arrive late. Try also not to arrive more than five or ten minutes early. If the interview involves a long journey, make time for a loo-stop *en route*. Don't arrive flustered and in a rush for the facilities. And don't plan to use their phones on arrival – or indeed at all.

Don't arrange to bring your spouse/parent/partner/dog to interviews. The effect is rarely favourable.

At the interview

Most folk agree that the interview process is an inefficient selection tool. Nearly all unstructured interviews are defective, and the benefits of some allegedly structured ones remain unproven. The problem for you is that the defects of the interview may prevent you being properly assessed, and some of your merits may not come across fully, or even at all. Similarly, you may not get a clear idea of the job or the organisation.

This does however give you an opportunity to manage the interview to your own advantage. First, be aware of what the interviewer is trying to find out about you – for example:

● Are your qualifications genuine and relevant?

■ Is your alleged experience genuine, relevant and as good as your CV suggests?

▲ What have you omitted from your CV or the application form which could be significant, for or against you?

● How intelligent are you, and is that adequate for the job?

● How good are your people skills? Could you train other people? Would you fit into a team?

● How good are your communication skills? Do you listen?

■ Are you honest – in self-disclosure, with your colleagues, with company money, property, services?

▲ Can you make an immediate contribution to the new job or would you need training?

Knowing what the interviewer needs to find out enables you to ensure that you provide it. The interviewer wants reassurance and confirmation of what you put in your CV and letter. If there is fresh, concrete evidence of your track record that modesty or space prevented you from putting into your paperwork, then your mentioning these at interview leaves the interviewer with the nice feeling that he or she has done a good job and has also proved you are better than your CV.

Interview basics

The following list is simply an aide-mémoire to help you avoid the worst pitfalls:

● Look at the interviewer.

■ Don't slouch.

▲ Always ask why the vacancy exists, why they have created the job and why they have gone outside to fill it. Ask too what early contribution the new incumbent can make. There may be short-term agendas that are not apparent from the formal job description.

● Answer the questions you are asked. You're not an MP!

● Try to make your answers concise, accurate and helpful.

● If you don't understand something, ask for clarification. If you fail to do so, the interviewer may think you're a non-listener or just stupid.

■ Stick to the point and don't go off on tangents.

▲ If you are asked hypothetical questions, try to recall something similar in your experience and make it clear this is the way you actually dealt successfully with the situation when you encountered it.

● Don't be chummy with the interviewer: don't use first names or try chat-up lines if he or she happens to attract you.

● Keep the emotion out of your leaving stories. Develop a brief, simple way of describing it, no matter how complex or unpleasant the situation really was.

● Be frank about your reasons for being on the market but don't rush to volunteer this information early on.

■ Never knock your previous employer. Find euphemisms if you have to that make it apparent you are being discreet.

Body language

It helps to be aware of the unspoken messages you are sending, and to be able to read your interviewer's. *Body Language* by Adrian Furnham in this series (London, IPD, 1999) is full of guidance but the following tips may help:

● Handshakes should be vertical, with neither hand under the other.

■ Bone-crusher handshakes are not assertive: they are offensive – as are wet-fish limp handshakes.

▲ An early smile is important.

● A bit of synchronised nodding and smiling when the other side says something interesting rings the changes on the necessary grunts and other affirmative noises.

● Mirroring the interviewer's posture – position of hands, legs etc – also indicates interest and empathy.

● It is better to keep arms and hands open rather than crossed defensively over the body or playing with hair, ears etc.

■ Try to focus on the interviewer's face, looking at or between the eyes, not dipping to cleavage etc.

▲ Leaning forward slightly, towards the interviewer, implies interest.

● Sitting to one side, rather than face to face across a desk or open space, is best because it appears less confrontational.

● Be aware that the higher seat offers a more commanding position, so aim for an equal level.

All these tips may appear trivial but, used subtly, they will have a quietly favourable impact. (Practise observing other people you know well in non-interview situations and try out some of the above ideas to monitor the difference they make.)

Tests and work samples

Many interviews are supplemented by tests, exercises, and work samples. These are an attempt to provide more reliable filtering of candidates. The basic ones you are likely to encounter, apart from the ubiquitous psychometric tests, include such skills tests as typing tests or in-tray exercises.

Because these are overt, you simply tackle them to the best of your ability. If you are worried about the outcome of psychometric tests or profiles, remind yourself that the beauty of these is that you cannot possibly fail! Simply answer as honestly as you can – and make sure you receive full feedback from the results afterwards. (It is unethical for this not to be provided. The information is your property and you have full rights to it.)

Closing the interview

By the end of the interview you should have a clearer idea of what the job entails – the responsibilities, reporting lines, prospects and so on. You should also know more about the organisation, especially the part you would be working in. As a result, you should know whether you still want to be considered for the job and have some idea of whether you are likely to be on the shortlist for the next stage.

Most competent interviewers will volunteer the information about what happens next, what the time-frame is, what you should expect etc as they draw the interview to a close. If they don't, it's reasonable to ask, politely.

In the car or on the train immediately after the interview, note down your impressions and any questions that remain unanswered. These impressions, captured while your memory of the meeting is fresh, may save you from making a bad move. And the questions will give you the basis for deepening the conversation when you get to the next stage.

7 after the interview

By the time you sit down for the interview, more than half the battle is won. But not all. When, some days later, they can't even remember what you looked like, there may be little except the original paperwork to help them choose between you and the others they saw. (Always assume that there are other candidates in play: it concentrates the mind wonderfully.) But don't despair. Following up effectively afterwards can make a significant contribution to your prospects.

The follow-up letter

If at all possible, ensure that they have given you a task to do after the interview, or volunteer to do something. Then write to the interviewer. Send them anything you promised to send them, and do it promptly so that they have a chance to register that you deliver the goods on time!

Don't simply write to thank them for the interview – that is tacky! Your wrap-up letter enables you to include details about specific points that came out in the interview but which modesty or lack of space forced you to omit from your earlier paperwork. Provide factual information to fill any gaps you think there may have been.

Your deeper understanding of the new employer's current problems may now enable you to indicate how specific bits of your experience should make you an instant contributor. Your aim here is to give reassurance about your suitability for the job – and to add to your credibility.

Claiming expenses

If you make travel expense claims during the recruitment process, take care that they are reasonable and agreed beforehand. If there are any problems, make sure that you have chatted discreetly with the recruiter's secretary to see whether they mind your coming by air or by sleeper, or staying overnight. Don't ask for first-class travel, high car-mileage rates or gourmet subsistence levels. And always include receipts if possible.

Look after your referees

Referees are people who are doing you a favour. Remember to ask them nicely before giving their names to anyone. Don't just automatically put them on your CV. Offer them as and when requested by a potential employer and keep them in the picture.

Brief your referees. If a specific slice of your experience is important for a particular vacancy, ensure that at least one of your referees knew you during that period. Nothing is worse than a friendly referee who is on your side but, when they find out what the job specification is, cannot in any honesty say that they can vouch for your ability in that area.

Don't forget to thank them, and keep them posted on your progress – anything less could make them feel exploited and taint the process.

Practise patience

Don't harass the interviewer. Don't bombard him or her with phone calls demanding progress reports and up-dates. Even the most favoured candidate can lose pole position this way. Remember, it's still a competition until somebody wins. You want to do everything in your power to ensure that the somebody is you!

8 negotiating the offer

It's happened. They ring – or write – and make you an offer. Wonderful. At last!

Hold it right there. You must not accept straight away the offer as it stands. You need time to think, and then you must negotiate. This is important. It is now that you have the best chance to secure the best possible framework for the new job – and that includes the structure of the job, the job title and the conditions, as well as the rewards package. It's at the point when you come under offer, or begin serious discussions on the likely content of such an offer, that you enter the most crucial period of the process.

Your objectives

You should already have a clear idea of what you want to achieve. There are several possible objectives:

● to get the best possible deal for yourself

■ to clarify any spoken but unwritten promises that the other side may later forget, or remember but renege on

▲ to maintain or enhance the other side's respect for you even when you are pushing to go beyond the original offer

● to keep the offer open until you want to accept it or reject it.

Bear in mind that the same discussion may be going on with one or more of the other candidates. And even if it is not, the window of opportunity won't remain open for ever.

Unless you get acceptance (expressed or implied) of your haggling, the other side may well pull the rug out just when you think you are near to final agreement.

Ensuring effective communication

Good communication is paramount. Employers may forget, or sometimes even not know, that someone on their team has given you more time to think things through. You must bridge that gap, preferably in writing, to keep the process going.

Never forget that the deal is more important to you than to them. It is up to you to ensure that there is proper communication. Tell the truth about your current situation and any other offers. It is much easier (saves you trying to remember what version you told whom) and usually much more convincing.

Remember that everything is negotiable. Consider whether trade-offs are possible or whether you can ask for the certainty of future benefits to compensate for the lack of flexibility on current ones. Steering a conversation round to something that would look pushy in writing can make your requests appear more acceptable.

And don't forget to massage their corporate ego and personal self-esteem at all times by reminding them that you think they're wonderful.

The things on your list for discussion, or even to put in writing at some stage, are likely to include the following:

● telling them you are very interested in working for them – even excited by the offer

■ but you wonder whether some minor modifications are possible in the package

▲ because…

There must always be a credible and honourable reason, otherwise it will just look like an 'I wanna' or 'Gimme!'

○ Good reasons will usually be because you want to get the job done properly. This can cover everything from a directorship to a minor change in job title, status or budget.

☐ Less-good reasons, but still important, will be about the fairness of the package in relation to your true worth, past rewards, need for motivation, outgoings or cost of living on their patch.

● Finally, get them to record in writing (or at least note) your restatement of any promises made at earlier meetings.

Avoiding backfires

Good communication is not just a question of timing or filling worrisome gaps. At each step you must think how your disclosures will be interpreted – or misinterpreted, and what precisely the reactions may be.

Being economical with the truth is likely to be counterproductive. So is playing hard to get. The ploy 'I've received a better offer – can you improve yours?' often backfires, producing:

● grudging consideration and cooling of relations

■ a derisory increase in the offer

▲ automatic rejection of your request

● complete withdrawal of the offer.

If you have developed a reasonable relationship with the future employer, and you have in fact received a better offer, set up a convenient meeting and go and talk through the problem.

Make it clear to the first firm that you still think they are terrific but that the other firm is different. Specify in which ways. Indicate where the other firm's offer is better and point out what is important to you – more money, comfort etc – from their offer. Say, if it's true, that you prefer their (the first firm's) offer, but that your decision would be easier if they could move closer to the other's.

Don't put a gun to their heads. You could ask what they would feel would be equitable. Or ask whether future rewards could be forecast, ie guaranteed, more clearly. This implies (you could even say it explicitly) that you are confident that by then they will know that you are worth the money.

Always summarise where you think you've got to, what has been agreed so far, and what loose ends remain to be dealt with. When you feel you have reached the buffers and you're achieving nothing more, take a break and come back fresh. If it's the end of the line and they won't budge far enough, shake hands on it and explain fairly why you're turning down their offer. And don't slam the door. They may need a day or two to reconsider.

9 acceptance and after

Congratulations! All that hard work was worth it. You have now accepted that great new job, negotiated satisfactory terms and got confirmation in writing. Phew!

But don't relax just yet. The next steps may make the difference in how difficult it will be when you come to repeat the job-search process in the future. It is time to pay your dues and say goodbye.

Saying 'thank you'

Whom should you thank? Everyone who helped you land this job:

- the people at the agency or consultancy who supported you, interviewed you and put your name forward

- the people you networked with whose leads led to this job

- anyone else who helped in any way.

It is courteous to assure people, where it is appropriate (for example in the agency or consultancy), that in future you will recommend them to others. It is even more courteous actually to do so!

How should you thank them? Orally or in writing, depending on how much they did to help. 'Not much' warrants a brief, polite phone call; 'very significantly' deserves a real thank-you letter.

Keeping people posted

Now is the time to publicise your good news. Not only is it good PR, it is also courteous to inform people who may have been keeping an eye out for a likely opportunity for you that now they can stand down.

You will want to include all the people on your network whom you contacted, any of their contacts whom you spoke to, the agencies you signed on with and any consultancies or counsellors who were involved in your search. In fact, you should include everyone you involved in the search who was not directly related to the final successful appointment.

This group of people deserves a genuine thank-you for the help they were able to provide. You should personalise your letter, if possible, to mention anything specific that was particularly helpful. It is thoughtful to offer *your* help in return should it ever be relevant to them or to someone they know. Networks require reciprocity to flourish, and it is wise to prime the pump when you are able. Who knows when you'll need it again?

Saying goodbye

There are temptations in the leaving process. If parting is not sweet sorrow but sheer delight, you may be tempted to swing from the boardroom chandelier and spray the chairman's Jaguar with yellow paint to match its owner's character, or at least tell everyone what you think of them – not least your immediate boss.

Don't. One day, you may need a reference from the person you were just about to insult. Worse, in the future when the firm is unrecognisable under new ownership, you may even find yourself applying to that person for a job. And worst of all, you may decide you made a mistake and want to go back.

Always leave a job in such a way that it enhances your reputation. This means quietly, graciously and, where required, generously. They may have done you wrong but you have no need to compound the error. Your letter of resignation should be factual, courteous and brief. It should always be inoffensive. Now is not the time to score points. Remember, if you offend people on the way up, they may be the people you need on the way down. And that letter remains on record in your file. Leave no skeletons...

Any celebrations of the new job with colleagues should be discreetly off-site where possible. And any expressions of regret should at least appear to be genuine! Your real friends know the inside story. Nobody else matters.

0 if they reject...

You won't get every job you apply for. Rejection, therefore, is something none of us can avoid. But we differ in how well we handle it. The first rule of rejection is: don't complain.

Why should your experience be any different from anyone else's? It is a buyer's market, and each employer has the luxury of choice. That means that 99 per cent of applicants for each job will be rejected. Recognising this simple fact of life will enable you to come to terms with the understandable frustration and depression that threaten as what looked like yet another good prospect slips from your grasp.

So, no sour grapes. Send no whingeing, whining letters. Instead, tackle the situation in a professional manner which leaves a good impression – and then get back to the drawing-board with due humility and elicit a second opinion from someone who is not totally besotted with you in order to identify where your presentation or 'product' fell short of the ideal.

Staying in the frame

You've had the 'Thank you but no thank you' letter and you assume they've offered the job to someone else. But don't back away just yet. There's many a slip between cup and lip, and today's preferred candidate may withdraw, negotiate so outrageously that they drop him, or get run over by a bus!

Write back and be gracious. Say thank you, it was very interesting, you would have liked to work with them... Mention that you still feel there was a very good match between you and the employer's known needs. If the rejection letter specified why you have been dropped, and you know you can counter that, mention it persuasively. You could win yourself a position as the first reserve. It might also help to suggest other ways they might be able to use you, now or in the future. Sign off positively, to leave a warm impression on the reader – and leave it there. They won't forget.

Keeping your allies

To get to the stage you are now in, you have probably put considerable effort into building up a network of allies – consultants, agencies, people you used to work for, target-employers who have responded in a friendly way and so on. It is crucial that you keep them in the picture and working for you.

Write and thank the ones who have been of help. Mention that the job-search continues and emphasise the positive aspects of your current situation (for example, second interviews, final shortlist of three). And, most importantly, don't whinge. Stay cheerful and sound confident. And make it worth their while reading your letter by mentioning any interesting titbits of industry information that you've picked up that you can pass on without being indiscreet. It may even produce a friendly phone call...

Making improvements

One positive approach you can take to the setback of rejection is to work at making yourself more marketable. This can cover a wide range of possibilities, from fairly superficial things – such as updating your wardrobe (a new interview suit, maybe?), improving your grooming, visiting your dentist, even simply getting a haircut – to dealing with deep-rooted behaviour patterns, such as inattention or habitual interrupting.

If asked (and assured that you won't retaliate), best friends and spouses *will* tell you what could be improved. The need to smarten up your act may even motivate you to deal with things like smoking, overeating and heavy drinking, in which case you will reap significant long-term benefits.

Now could be a good time to brush up on skills such as computer knowledge and foreign languages, or to get much-needed qualifications. Your local library will be well stocked with resources to help you, and employers are likely to be more impressed with people who have used their time productively than those who simply vegetated in front of the TV. *Learning for Earning* by Eric Parsloe and Caroline Allen in this series (London, IPD, 1999) will help you to find out how you can accelerate your learning and discover more about developing your skills to increase your market value.

Managing the process

Some careers advisers suggest that looking for a better job is itself a full-time job. This is rarely true. You do need to manage yourself and your time when you're out of work, however. You need to make the best use of the time available and the effort you put into the job-search. And you need to keep yourself mentally and physically in good shape to help yourself fight the frustration and depression that will surely threaten you at various times.

You need to set realistic targets, do your research and be well prepared. Then try to be as cheerful as circumstances permit. You will need patience – but, with the right tools, techniques and tactics, you should succeed.

in conclusion

Job-hunting is horrid, and especially horrid if it's been forced upon you rather than entered into voluntarily from the safety of a current and apparently stable on-going position. But there are ways to make it more bearable and more likely to produce fruit sooner than later.

The key points to remember are these:

- Employers are the people who have created, or may have created, or may be prepared to create the job you want.

- Consultants and agencies are the middlemen – the agents of the employers.

- Employers are the better target.

- You need to approach employers differently from the way in which you approach the middlemen. It may be acceptable to omit some information (eg salary) when writing to a potential employer, but don't do this with consultants. They need enough information to be able to see the match between you and future vacancies.

- A substantial majority of all applicants for all jobs apply badly, and at least half shouldn't have bothered to apply at all. If you concentrate on jobs where you are genuinely relevant and you apply well, you may be able to put yourself in the top 10 per cent of applicants at a stroke.

● We all have doubts about our suitability for a job and worry about the weaknesses in our CV. The trick is turning what we have done to advantage.

■ Know what you need and what you have to offer.

▲ Do what is asked of you – send back application forms and comply precisely with reply instructions. Provide all the information they ask for in the way they ask. Co-operate!

● Make every document a marketing document.

● Get somebody else to check everything you send out – not the copy, but the original, and *before* you seal that envelope and post it.

● At interview, be yourself – but your best self.

■ Everything you do during your job-search is a work sample. Do everything that you do excellently at every stage of the process.

▲ Keep your network alive – you may need it again!

Finally, if you take all this advice, there is hope. Merely thinking about the impression you are creating (without doing this too obviously) gives you a deserved advantage over all the other applicants competing against you.

Know that you are probably better than any internal candidates. If there was someone who was an obvious choice, his or her employer would not be advertising. (This does not apply to a public-sector job where external advertising is a compulsory part of the process.)

Have a look at the junk mail you receive every week. Unconvincing? You need to make *your* document convincing so that the reader feels comfortable about and understands your relevance, and even wants to meet you before he or she finishes reading your letter.

Do keep in mind the people you are competing against. This is not a one-horse race. Try to do yourself justice, so that anyone reading your paperwork can do so too.

Remember that you do not exist for the employer until your papers have made you credible and interesting. Right now may be your last chance of checking that they fulfil this crucial task. Ask someone who is not so besotted with or beholden to you that they won't tell the plain truth. What's the impact of your CV? Does the covering letter really work for you and make the reader want to look at your CV?

By now, both documents should be about 90 per cent right. But there's still time for a last ruthless edit to tighten them up, or even add a little more emphasis to the things that make you stand out from the crowd.

Never forget: the name of the game is marketing, and you are the product. The jobs are out there. Go for it – and good luck!

With over 90,000 members, the **Institute of Personnel and Development** is the largest organisation in Europe dealing with the management and development of people. The IPD operates its own publishing unit, producing books and research reports for human resource practitioners, students, and general managers charged with people-management responsibilities.

Currently there are some 160 titles covering the full range of personnel and development issues. The books have been commissioned from leading experts in the field and are packed with the latest information and guidance on best practice.

For free copies of the IPD Books Catalogue, please contact the publishing department:

Tel.: 020-8263 3387
Fax: 020-8263 3850
E-mail: publish@ipd.co.uk
Web: www.ipd.co.uk

Orders for books should be sent to:

Plymbridge Distributors
Estover
Plymouth
Devon
PL6 7PZ

(Credit card orders) Tel.: 01752 202 301
Fax: 01752 202 333

Upcoming titles in the *Management Shapers* series

Publication: September 1999

The Manager as Coach and Mentor
Eric Parsloe
ISBN 0 85292 803 3

Persuasive Reports and Proposals
Andrew Leigh
ISBN 0 85292 809 2

Presentation Skills
Suzy Siddons
ISBN 0 85292 810 6

Other titles in the *Management Shapers* series

All titles are priced at £5.95 (£5.36 to IPD members)

The Appraisal Discussion

Terry Gillen

Shows you how to make appraisal a productive and motivating experience for all levels of performer. It includes:

- assessing performance fairly and accurately

- using feedback to improve performance

- handling reluctant appraisees and avoiding bias

- agreeing future objectives

- identifying development needs.

1998 96 pages   ISBN 0 85292 751 7

Asking Questions

Ian MacKay
(Second Edition)

Will help you ask the 'right' questions, using the correct form to elicit a useful response. All managers need to hone their questioning skills, whether interviewing, appraising or simply exchanging ideas. This book offers guidance and helpful advice on:

- using various forms of open question – including probing, simple interrogative, opinion-seeking, hypothetical, extension and precision etc

- encouraging and drawing out speakers through supportive statements and interjections

- establishing specific facts through closed or 'direct' approaches

- avoiding counter-productive questions

- using questions in a training context.

1998 96 pages   ISBN 0 85292 768 1

Assertiveness

Terry Gillen

Will help you feel naturally confident, enjoy the respect of others and easily establish productive working relationships, even with 'awkward' people. It covers:

- understanding why you behave as you do and, when that behaviour is counter-productive, knowing what to do about it

- understanding other people better

- keeping your emotions under control

- preventing others' bullying, flattering or manipulating you

- acquiring easy-to-learn techniques that you can use immediately

- developing your personal assertiveness strategy.

1998 96 pages   ISBN 0 85292 769 X

Constructive Feedback

Roland and Frances Bee

Practical advice on when to give feedback, how best to give it, and how to receive and use feedback yourself. It includes:

- using feedback in coaching, training, and team motivation

- distinguishing between criticism and feedback

- 10 tools for giving constructive feedback

- dealing with challenging situations and people.

1998 96 pages   ISBN 0 85292 752 5

The Disciplinary Interview

Alan Fowler

This book will ensure that you adopt the correct procedures, conduct productive interviews and manage the outcome with confidence. It includes:

- understanding the legal implications

- investigating the facts and presenting the management case

- probing the employee's case and defusing conflict

- distinguishing between conduct and competence

- weighing up the alternatives to dismissal.

1998 96 pages   ISBN 0 85292 753 3

Leadership Skills

John Adair

Will give you confidence and guide and inspire you on your journey from being an effective manager to becoming a leader of excellence. Acknowledged as a world authority on leadership, Adair offers stimulating insights into:

- recognising and developing your leadership qualities

- acquiring the personal authority to give positive direction and the flexibility to embrace change

- acting on the key interacting needs – to achieve your task, build your team, and develop its members

- transforming the core leadership functions such as planning, communicating and motivating into practical skills you can master.

1998 96 pages   ISBN 0 85292 764 9

Listening Skills

Ian MacKay

(Second Edition)

Improve your ability in this crucial management skill! Clear explanations will help you:

- ● recognise the inhibitors to listening

- ■ listen to what is really being said by analysing and evaluating the message

- ▲ interpret tone of voice and non-verbal signals.

1998 80 pages   ISBN 0 85292 754 1

Making Meetings Work

Patrick Forsyth

Will maximise your time (both before and during meetings), clarify your aims, improve your own and others' performance and make the whole process rewarding and productive. The book is full of practical tips and advice on:

- drawing up objectives and setting realistic agendas

- deciding the who, where, and when to meet

- chairing effectively – encouraging discussion, creativity and sound decision-making

- sharpening your skills of observation, listening and questioning to get your points across

- dealing with problem participants

- handling the follow-up – turning decisions into action.

1998 96 pages   ISBN 0 85292 765 7

Motivating People

Iain Maitland

Will help you maximise individual and team skills to achieve personal, departmental and, above all, organisational goals. It provides practical insights into:

- becoming a better leader and coordinating winning teams

- identifying, setting and communicating achievable targets

- empowering others through simple job improvement techniques

- encouraging self-development, defining training needs and providing helpful assessment

- ensuring that pay and workplace conditions make a positive contribution to satisfaction and commitment.

1998 96 pages   ISBN 0 85292 766 5

Negotiating, Persuading and Influencing

Alan Fowler

Develop the skills you need to manage your staff effectively, bargain successfully with colleagues or deal tactfully with superiors. Sound advice on:

- probing and questioning techniques
- timing your tactics and using adjournments
- conceding and compromising to find common ground
- resisting manipulative ploys
- securing and implementing agreement.

1998 96 pages   ISBN 085292 755 X

Working in Teams

Alison Hardingham

Looks at teamworking from the inside. It will give you valuable insights into how you can make a more positive and effective contribution – as team member or team leader – to ensure that your team works together and achieves together. Clear and practical guidelines are given on:

- understanding the nature and make-up of teams

- finding out if your team is on track

- overcoming the most common teamworking problems

- recognising your own strengths and weaknesses as a team member

- giving teams the tools, techniques and organisational support they need.

1998 96 pages   ISBN 0 85292 767 3